Maya Goes to Hospital

Written by Victoria Beech and the Paediatric Chaplaincy Network
Illustrated by Rhiannon Mollart

This is
Maya

Maya is listening to
a story about Jesus.

He tells his friends

he will
always
be with them.

Maya goes to bed.

She thanks Jesus for being with her.

Maya is playing with her toys.

Maya knows that

Jesus is with her.

Maya is at church.
She sings songs about Jesus' love.

Maya knows that Jesus is with her.

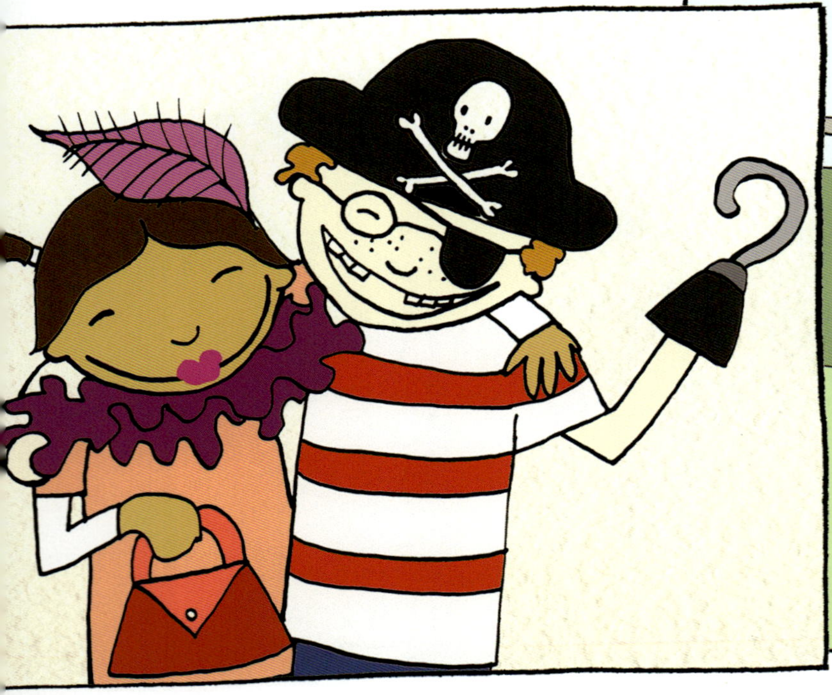
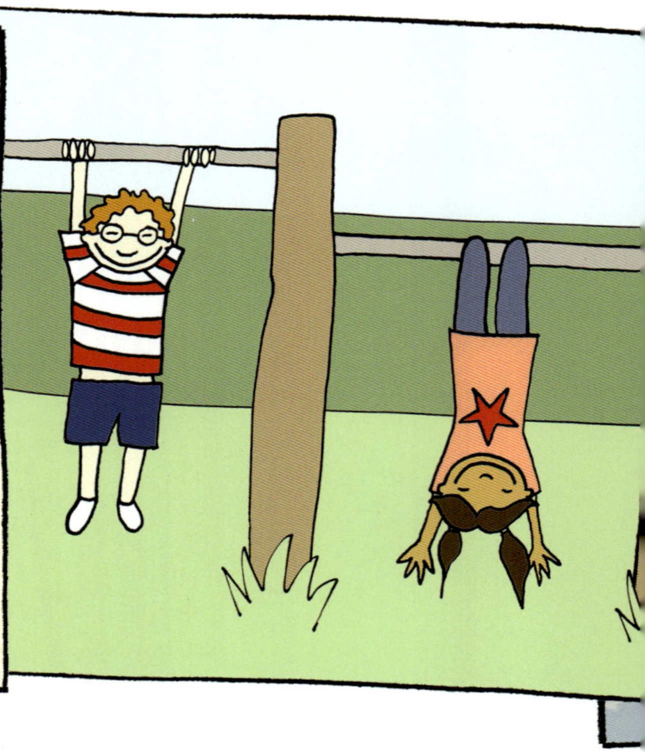

Maya is at Alex's house.

She has lots of **fun.**

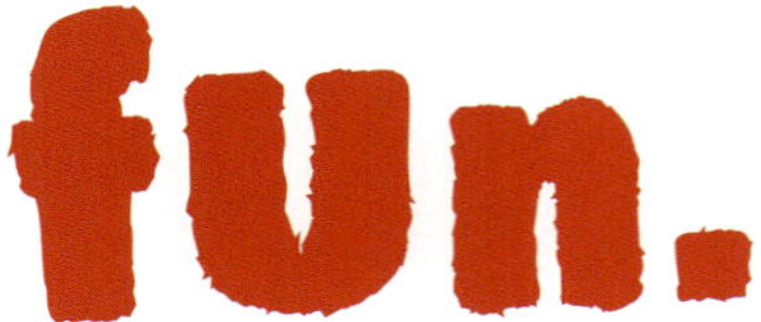

Maya knows that Jesus is with her.

Maya goes to hospital.

She has lots of questions.

will I be able to
play there?

will Alex be there?

can I take Rosie?

will it hurt?

when will I come home again?

who will
be there
with me?

Maya meets lots of new people at the hospital.

They are making her better.

Maya is a bit frightened.

She feels lonely.

what has she forgotten?

Maya remembers Jesus is with her.

She imagines Jesus in hospital clothes.

Maya leaves the hospital and says goodbye to the hospital people.

But not to Jesus.

WELCOME

Maya goes home.

She is happy.

Maya knows that
Jesus is with her.

HOME!

And he will be with her

wherever

she goes.*

* Bible verse from Matthew 28:20 CEV

Thank you for buying this book.

Jesus said to his friends just before he went back to heaven: 'I will be with you always, even until the end of the world.' (Matthew 28:20, Contemporary English Bible). This story uses these words as a springboard for thinking about Jesus being with us everywhere we go, even in hospital.

You might like to use this prayer: Thank you, Jesus, for being with me all the time.

How can I use this book with my child?

The book is intended for children aged three to seven. You might like to read the book to your child, asking him or her questions and talking about the pictures together. If your child can read, she or he may wish to read this book alone or with you, thinking about it and sharing thoughts with you.

What questions could I use to chat about things in this book?

- Can you count all the places Maya knows Jesus is with her?
- Do you know any songs about Jesus' love?
- What does Maya play with Alex? Who are your friends? What do you like doing with them?
- What do you think might be the answers to Maya's questions about hospital?
- If you had a dream about you and Jesus, what would it be like?

How should I answer my child's questions?

How much your child understands about his or her illness will depend on age and awareness of any physical changes. If your child asks questions, listen carefully to the words he or she uses and try to answer questions, giving the information asked for, keeping your answers reassuring, simple, honest, direct and consistent.

How can I use play to help my child?

Your child may find it helpful to express his or her fears and needs, using play. Play is how children make sense of the world around them, so it is important that they have the opportunity to play freely. During play you may find your child expresses strong emotions. It can be helpful to find words that describe the emotion such as 'big angry', 'little angry', 'grumpy', 'cross' and so on.

What about routines?

Even children who are poorly are likely to want to carry on doing the activities they usually enjoy. Routines are helpful for you, your child and for any other children you have.

What about my child's siblings?

Brothers and sisters will often be worried about their ill sibling and you may find it difficult to spend as much time together as a family. Brothers and sisters need:

- opportunities to express their feelings
- adults who will express their own emotions
- information about what is wrong with their sibling
- opportunities to play and enjoy activities they have previously shared with their sibling.

What about you?

If your child becomes ill, you will be carrying a considerable burden. Try to be kind and compassionate with yourself. It is important to maintain a sense of hope, not only for your children but also for yourself. Faith can provide enormous support and solace. You may find it difficult to pray. Try to find a place where you feel comfortable and safe and in a way that seems right for you to 'let go and let God'. It is amazing how many parents achieve a sense of hopefulness and talk about the grace they received so that they were able to cope.

Activities you might find helpful

- In the run-up to going to hospital, place sticky notes saying 'Jesus is with me' in some of the different places your child goes, and take some with you to hospital.
- Draw pictures of the different questions your child has about hospital and chat about them together.
- Chat with your child about the different places you each go to. Invent your own 'story' along these lines: You say: '[You child's name] goes to play group'. Your child says: '[Your child's name] knows that Jesus is with him/her.'

Resources and organisations

- **When you're Sick or in the Hospital** by Tom McGrath, published by One Caring Place, Indiana 2002.
- **The Broken Leg** by Leslie J Francis and Nicola M Slee, published by Christian Education - Teddy Horsley goes to hospital and meets Jesus in all the people who help when he hurts himself.
- **Topsy and Tim: Go to Hospital** by Jean Adamson and Gareth Adamson published by Ladybird 2010. Tim is a little nervous about going to hospital, but he soon finds out how nice the doctors and nurses are.

www.wellchild.org.uk WellChild helps sick children and their families manage the consequences of serious illness and complex health conditions.

www.sickchildrenstrust.org The Sick Child Trust provides high quality 'Home from Home' accommodation for families whose children are receiving hospital treatment for serious illness.

www.actionforsickchildren.org/index.asp?ID=152 Action for Sick Children was formed to ensure that sick children always receive the highest standard of care possible.

Notes